THE
Untold Story
OF *Jesus Christ,*
IN HIS OWN WORDS

LIA MOTIRAM

BALBOA.PRESS
A DIVISION OF HAY HOUSE

Balboa Press books may be ordered through booksellers or by contacting:

Balboa Press
A Division of Hay House
1663 Liberty Drive
Bloomington, IN 47403
www.balboapress.com
844-682-1282

Because of the dynamic nature of the Internet, any web addresses or links contained in this book may have changed since publication and may no longer be valid. The views expressed in this work are solely those of the author and do not necessarily reflect the views of the publisher, and the publisher hereby disclaims any responsibility for them.

The author of this book does not dispense medical advice or prescribe the use of any technique as a form of treatment for physical, emotional, or medical problems without the advice of a physician, either directly or indirectly. The intent of the author is only to offer information of a general nature to help you in your quest for emotional and spiritual well-being. In the event you use any of the information in this book for yourself, which is your constitutional right, the author and the publisher assume no responsibility for your actions.

Any people depicted in stock imagery provided by Getty Images are models, and such images are being used for illustrative purposes only. Certain stock imagery © Getty Images.

Print information available on the last page.

ISBN: 978-1-9822-5236-6 (sc)
ISBN: 978-1-9822-5257-1 (e)

Balboa Press rev. date: 08/14/2020

CONTENTS

ACKNOWLEDGEMENTS

I would like to thank God and Goddess I AM THAT I AM whom I called Lord God and Goddess All That Is. He and She are of Love and Light and Our Creator of the Universe and beyond. Since this is a patriarchal world, God has been the main underlying focus my entire life so far. I began my journey to find God at the age of 8. I thank You our Heavenly Father for being my support system when I didn't have any. You uplifted me and I am grateful. Your gift of Access to the Akashic Records is enormous and my Healing abilities as well. My love and Gratitude to you both. I love you.

I would like to thank the Lords of Akashic Records, Masters, Teachers and Guides for your life lessons, healing and your patience with me. You have taught me very important life lessons, and provided me with insightful information about my own life and for others. I appreciate all that you do, with love and Gratitude. Thank you for suggesting I take up Reiki and other modalities.

I would like to Thank my Archangel team, who helps and supports me in different ways, Archangel Michael, Archangel Raphael, Archangel Gabriel, Archangel Uriel. I would like to thank all the other Archangels and Angels as well. Thank you!

I would like to thank Jeshua Christ AKA Jesus Christ who gifted me his story of his life lived as Jesus Christ. I am truly honored to receive this story of your life. With enormous love and gratitude, I thank you.

I would like to thank Balboa Press for helping me publish this book, especially Michael March and Rebecca Clements and Staff who have been so helpful.

PORTRAIT OF JESHUA CHRIST called The Lamb and the Lion, on front cover is by Glenda Green, an accomplished artist with stories of her own who painted the actual likeness of Jeshua Christ aka Jesus Christ. He posed for her. Her story is in the book, *Love Without End* by Glenda Green. Please visit her website: https://inspiredorigination.com/

Glenda Green, this painting is beautiful and I am happy to receive it for the front cover. Thank you.

To My children, Thomas, Kristy and Brandon, remember when I told you often, that each one of you is special to me. All of you are like different colours of a rainbow. You all are unique and special in your own way. I love you Thomas, Kristy and Brandon- Mom

Blessings to All,

Lia K. Motiram

INTRODUCTION

My name is Lia Kalpana Motiram. I have always been a spiritual person since beginning of my journey to find God at the age of 7. This was a result of my first spiritual experience of an altered vision where my perception of everything around me increased hugely. Imagine that you were 6 inches tall and from that perspective you are looking at the street, the traffic lights buildings etc. That was my first vision which lasted 10 seconds. The next day I woke up and asked my Hindu mother to tell me about God and she said, "God dies and is born again." I was very upset when she said that, I replied, "God never dies, people die and are reborn. God never dies." How I knew this, I do not know. From that moment on, I went searching for God.

My search for God led me to Spiritual books like Seth Speaks and Seth Material and other Seth Books by Jane Roberts, then I moved on to read *Celestine Prophesies* by James Redfield, *Out on a Limb* by Shirley MacLaine and other books of hers like *The Camino*. Then my all time favourite books, *Conversations With God* by Neale Donald Walsch. I fell in love with God and wanted to come home to Heaven. I was not happy with my life by the time I began my 40th birthday. I had 3 very young children that needed me but my own personal life was intolerable to me. I wrote a letter to God asking for permission to come home. This was when He answered my prayers and said, "NO, finish your life." I didn't know it then, but my life had a purpose.

In 2002, I had a reading from an acquaintance of mine who was and is a student of the Akashic Records. I didn't know people could connect to the Akashic Records. Akashic Records are called Book Of Life in the Christian Bible. According to the Bible it holds the names of all those who are going to Heaven. But in actual fact, they are recordings of every thought, every word and behaviours or actions, that is written in energetic form inside your Akashic Records. Each one of us has an Akashic Records located in the Hall of Records in Heaven. They hold information regarding your current life and your past life lived.

Anyhow, my readings indicated that I was to become an Akashic Records Consultant. After the initial shock, as I never saw myself being psychic; I was science based having taken Electronics Engineering Technology as my career path at the age of 20. I submitted to an initiation of the Akashic Records and was given the gift of Clair Audience, where I can hear the voice of The Lords of Akashic Records, My Masters, Teachers and Loved Ones. Then they suggested that I take up Reiki Energy Healing. I did and became a Reiki Master.

One day I was talking to God and I asked him about Jesus Christ. Coming from a Hindu background and was more spiritual and Agnostic, I really didn't know all that much about Jesus Christ. So when I asked God about Jesus Christ, He send him to me. I was lying in bed on Saturday morning in 2005 Christmas Eve, when I sensed Jesus Christ standing beside my bed. Then he spoke and said he had a Christmas Gift for me. Then he said, "on the first Monday morning 2006 at 11:00, sit in front of your computer and I will give you my life story as Jesus Christ."

I did what he said. I was wondering why he would give me his life story because of my Hindu background and I didn't know much about him except that he was crucified on the cross. He said, "you are a clear channel." what that meant was that, I had no biases or resistance to his words, as I knew hardly anything about him. He suggested that I watch the Passion of Christ by Mel Gibson but I refused, as it was too violent. And I couldn't bear to watch him suffer.

I didn't even know what questions to ask, so I decided to be his Scribe ie secretary, and write down everything he said Word for Word.

Its interesting to note, that my experience entering data into the computer came from a job at a call centre for Ford Motor Company. When customers called in, I entered everything they said for their records. That job ended in February 2002. I held that job for 3 years so I had lots of practice typing word for word what the customers were saying.

I also had lots of practice writing word for word from the Heavenly Lords of Akashic Records, Masters, Teachers and Guides. This is what they said, "Definition of The Messiah is required. A **Messiah** is an Aramaic word for **The Chosen One of God and Goddess Holy Light and Love.**" the term, "**Second Coming** is the same exact person arriving reincarnated. The Second Coming means the same as the Messiah. **This book is to open their eyes and awaken their hearts, minds, Soul Spirits senses to what is reality; and <u>Who decides whose experiences are the truth?</u>**"

This book is Shocking with Revelations after Revelations. I hope you will experience what I experienced when Jesus Christ told me his story. WOW!!!!!!!

CHAPTER 1

My Birth

"**B**ehold a child is born in Bethlehem to you,** was told to Mary, my mother when she was a mere age of 14 years. She being a child herself, was impregnated by a Jewish Priest who called himself Archangel Gabriel from their First Church of Jerusalem.

These words were mere words to her, as they had zero meaning, but devastatingly accurate words when her mother heard from her lips who had impregnated her one and only child at that time frame.

Josephine, Mary's mother soon distraught at her daughter's upcoming birth prayed to Our Lord God for assistance wondering who and how she, a mere child can carry an infant who is suppose to be born out of wedlock. The voice of Our Father immediately replied to her, "**Hold your tongue and not chastise the Father for gifting her only child with the birth of the One Messiah who has been foretold by Elijah Prophets.**" Still she queried and was scared, frightened to tell others of who had done this to her only daughter. When Our Father replied, "**all in good time.**"

None believed she was telepathically communicating with Our Lord God All That Is. They all felt that Mary was either raped or some other such nonsense. Those at the Church of Jerusalem refused to defend her story or corroborate with why and how they could do such a thing. Their only excuse was to chastise Mary for being loose and knowingly desiring a young Priest who is just earning his right of passage. Others knew what this message was told to Josephine by Our Lord God All That Is, though they chose to not believe it so. "These were choice words from Our Lord, Our God," she exclaimed to deaf ears, as all know or think they know this was some bizarre cover up to hide her daughter's indiscretion.

Once the pregnancy was revealed as she could no longer hide the fact, Her daughter was upset as her figure was being changed by this bundle of energy, she called a baby. Then her father Ben Joseph allowed her to leave her home to visit a distance cousin of hers called Elizabeth who was also with child, so she can familiarize herself with all those womanly ways that she must take care of, to have a healthy infant born to her.

It was during this time frame when Our Lord God has spoken to Elizabeth to advise her she should expect Mary in her household and to show her the ways of a woman with child, teach her about being pregnant, as she had children of her own prior to this pregnancy.

Once My mother Mary arrived, Elizabeth found her at least 6 months pregnant, she exclaimed to Our Father, "how can a child so small hold such an infant as this Holy child of God?" When He replied, **"she has the capacity to love the most and it is her love that blesses this child she carries for all others to have and to hold, for richer for poorer until death do each of you part."** "No matter," thought Elizabeth, "I am going to keep her here until she labours."

Unfortunately, Our Lord God had other plans for Mary. No sooner than she had learned sufficiently regarding her pregnancy, she was to return to Jerusalem to rebuild her life. What that entailed was the wedding between her and Joseph was take hold. This meeting was denounced by his mother and father from the beginning, only Joseph had seen Mary and was smitten by her. He was told by God to keep her as his bride, such that, this child she carries will have a wedded father to come home to. His ideal bride should have been a virgin, as that is what is expected; relentlessly he pursued his bride until she gave in near the very end of her pregnancy.

By this time frame all decreed by governments that any subsequent births must be registered at the place of original births of the mother in keeping with records of lineage. So off they went to Bethlehem to register their births and deaths. She road on a pony as all was provided for her to be as comfortable as possible. Though they lacked much in terms of wares, however, they had what they needed the most, each other's love so strong that none were able to break them apart.

Upon reaching Bethlehem, they resorted to finding a safe, warm place for Mary to rest and relax until Our Lord Jesus' arrival, as the name had already been given by Our Father Lord God until such time as he arrives. The one and only place they were able to find was in a barn to which they became angered by Our Father's neglect of her and this child as they by now had sequestered, this child belong to the world, not just them. They then found out that they were better off in the warm barn with all the other animals, though they thought it smelled unpleasant it was the quietest place to rest and relax given the amount of wheat shafts and such that was gathered there.

Then a sudden stirring occurred and the child was born to Mary and Joseph, just after the barman's wife appeared to provide them with a cloth and towels and such for her comfort. She became the midwife to deliver this child to my mother Mary who lay there quietly without so much pain as other women had endured. "This pregnancy was a breeze," she thought, until such time as she had another child, when she knew how gifted I was in my arrival.

I was called the Holy child by all those who had witnessed my birth and decreed that I was special, so special that my powers were to become acknowledged by all those who seen me grow up. The problem occurred when I was 9 and began to show off my knowledge in spirituality. Though others had seen and known my intelligence level, though they had argued with my father Joseph regarding my overtures, that I am to be seen and heard from not. He decided that it was time for me to learn lessons of the spiritual kind that only the Church in Jerusalem can provide me with. There I engaged and learned the Kabbalah, thought to provide me with sufficient spiritual knowledge. Once I had mastered the Kabbalah, he then thought to send me off to far away place referred to as 'the old lands.' now called India. This thought had occurred to him without his thinking about it, so much so that he was drawn to anything that came from there; when he heard of a mystic Yogi who can do all sorts of interventions, even healing those who had the misfortune to lose an eye or limb so that they would some how reappear in perfect harmony with all things natural. This intrigued my father so much so that he himself, as the days grew long, come to find out where he resides and asked him to Educate me when I was 13 years of age.

My separation from my parents were the most difficult time for me to endure. By this time I had brothers and sisters to whom I adored. Many of them came for a visit from time to time but still the aloneness that I felt was more than I can bear. This Yogi to whom I won't name, as it is far too long of a name to recall, had transpired to teach me how to meditate until I cannot feel my senses any longer. This took years of practice. Unbeknownst to me, at that time frame, that I would require these teachings, when I would become a man of 37 years of age.

I had spent many nights alone in a small house similar to a hut enclosed from others who would come by and peer in from time to time. I would be given all that I required by the Yogi, who by that time had desired to share a known secret that all Yogis had come to realize. That once you reach Nirvana, for those who choose to learn meditation, there is no need for you to return to this life. My immediate desire was to leave this hellhole of a place they called India and return to my family and if that was impossible then I would choose to meditate until death had taken my life. But that was a choice Our Lord God had so denied me. I meditated until I could do no more than to stand on my feet as I could only feel less then. My entire body had become so numb of feeling to the point where this Yogi had injected a known substance within my flesh, that I could no longer feel, even pain did not vanquish me.

All of a sudden I received a genuine call for me to return to visit my relatives and my loved ones who were residing in Jerusalem at this time. I was elated. This time I had turned 18 years of age and to be recognized as a full-grown man. My father Joseph, had made sufficient wealth to have me come in style, as I was told to remove my clothing and wear the modern clothes of a young man who would meet seniors like myself to grow out my days with for a while. But this cause for concern had taken a much lovelier twist within me. There in front of my eyes as I sit in Jerusalem, lay hold a beautiful maid to whom I was smitten at first sight. She became by bride-to-be at a tender age of 18.

Unbeknownst to her family though, I had received blessings from Our Father Lord God who had explained to me the facts of life, as my urges to become a man and have enjoyable sex became much too much of an urge for me to bear, without some form of outlet. She and I had taken each other in our arms and besides our bodies, ensuring that I did not impregnate her accordingly. We had our ways as Our Lord God had told to me, as did this Yogi on how not to impregnate a woman.

We cherished each other joyously, until one day we were caught by her 3 brothers in a compromised fashion and was told by her parents to leave me alone and had her committed into marrying the first person who had proposed to her, unknowing she had been sacrificed by me already. To this day, I laugh, but what became of this unholy alliance between her and her betrothed, was something to write about for sure. We were engaged in Our Lord God's eyes but they had her engaged to another person, as she had come from a richly family who had given her all she had desired. Her name was Mary Magdalene from the house of Benjamin. They felt that my presence was not to be enjoyed by her, even though she begged to wed me. They chose me to be a bastard child who had no father and therefore shall not wed their first and famously wealthy daughter.

When this news came to my ears, I immediately proposed to her and asked for her hand in marriage, much to her family's dismay. My proposal caused a huge furor over at their house and they denounced their only daughter to be none other than a whore in those terms.

We had a small ceremony to which all my family members came and those who chose to stay away including her parents chose to keep her at a distance until such time as our first child arrived at our doorstep. This means she was pregnant with our first child who we named Benjamin like my father before him. He was called Joseph Junior, later on in his life. Then her mother came secretly to ensure her daughter's safety and joy all abound in her when she first laid eyes on her mother. Then slowly they accepted this marriage and then began my career as a teacher, as they so often called upon me.

Though my Education on the Vedics taught me a great deal of spiritual lessons, these lessons were placed on deaf ears and they soon denounced my knowledge and ability to reinterpret the Book of Moses, they had so often quoted to me over and over and over again. These notes were used and reused and each time those who misunderstood those readings required that I re-educate myself into believing their mistaken interpretations, rather than share my own correct versions. This they took as an idealism of a young man to whom they ought to re-teach and then they chose me to become a Rabbi, just so they can shame me into neglecting my earlier teachings and reacquaint me with their misguided ones.

By this time I was age 27, when my teaching became widely known and accepted even by those who chose not to listen to me but couldn't understand their own Rabbi's version, as common sense was something general population had available to them, but those learned ones refused to see their own illogical rational reasoning and accept those faiths that made zero sense to them, as it is occurring now in science and in theology, to this day and age, those learned one blindside themselves removing logic and rational reasoning from their mental constructions of their mind.

When I am seeing such mental attitudes, I revert back to my earlier days and re-teach those students to whom I was given and though none had ever argued my position of logic and reasoning, this did nothing to sway those who truly believed in garbage thought versus my own, that made so much sense, when placed against their experiences. Those who chose to follow the other's paths and advice found to their often dismay, it makes no sense at all given their personal experiences. In those days, Rabbis took what was taught to them without questioning the validity or common sense rational reasoning against the backdrop of their lives lived.

It amazes me even now that I think about it, how did they ever agree to call me a Rabbi since I had argued with their illogic of it all and they had zero answers for me. So instead of fighting me, they caused me to leave their school of thought and hoped that I would see my wayward ways. Of course this did not come to pass at all, so they sent me here and there with my wife hoping upon hope that I would refuse what I had been taught at my school in India by a Teacher who had taken a liking to me and had me study the Vedas.

These Vedas were powerful teaching tools and unlike their own interpretations, all power of Lord God were removed from their biblical books and became tainted with misnomers and biases of all those men who chose to write their own misguided interpretations of the events that occurred. As this has also occurred to the King James Version of the Bible and all those other so called biblical books of other faiths and religions. The power of Lord God has been besmirched with other's thoughts and biases losing what they once were, a powerful book on how life should be led and guided along the paths to righteousness for His names sake. Only the Vedas kept themselves pure even now, not one word was rewritten, as many have written their own books and theories surrounding their interpretations, only the Vedas remains pure. And that is how it should be. You can rewrite your versions but keep the original in its purest form.

Telepathy is a powerful tool as this book is being written the exact same way as those books were written. Though now they are besmirched and impure and incorrect. Love Rules in all of us. So if there is violence in any of these books, then these are not the writings of the Heaven's plane but some wayward person who had anger and prejudice. Be warned and examine accordingly.

Qur'an is a thought that comes from me, Lord Jesus Christ, the Authorship was re-written by none other than humans who agreed not to disclose the original writer of those manuscripts. As you can see many truths are being told to you.

I am now revealing all truths in this book due to the course of history that must be revealed. All religion is pure thought at first until man who becomes egoic in their nature decide to excise whatever is not palpable to them for the sake of controlling other people. That is the main reason why the Roman Catholic Church had refused ordinary persons to read and understand their biblical books, as their thoughts and lives lived would take control of who they think they are, not who they truly are.

I realize I am going back and forth between the present and the past only I choose to reveal much truths in this time frame.

CHAPTER 2

◆

My Earlier Teaching Career

By this time my authoritative relationship with my students became severe and all those other Rabbis could not compete with my teaching methods and the idea of having students sit quietly meditating is something they still do not do. They thought it was a waste of time and energy to allow young students to sit quietly staring at a candle and imagine their world outside of themselves be inside of themselves, as that is what I taught them. Since this is unheard of in Judaism the religion, they refused to see the validity of this exercise as they could not, nor would they agree to try it for themselves.

What they thought was, I was tainting their religion with garbage from another race of people to which they all felt did not completely understand who and what the Jews were all about. This prejudice is apparent even now, that none thought to examine pure thought other than their own.

This lead to my leaving the Jewish faith completely and turning my back on the same people I used to think of as my own race. By this time they thought me a heretic and banned me from teaching my subjects completely. Not knowing what more I can do, I turned to Mary

9

Magdalene to support me in my time of indecision. We then came to a decision that we could start our own school of thought.

When we reached this decision, it was a time for doing great things as there were not many wars in this time period and we were able to view what we can do to merge our people to a better understanding of God and our religion, Judaism. With God's help, I established our first forum for those who would enjoy teaching in our School of Christian Faith. Christian for my Title as the Christ Child, as I was known in my town of Jerusalem. Though my Title did nothing to bring down this faith called Judaism. As it is, my form of teaching became a threat to those learned ones who thought I was converting followers of the Jewish faith, as many agreed with my teachings which caused them to leave the Jewish faith behind them.

We attracted many Romans to our school of thought as well, since we balanced their feminine Goddess with our masculine God. Equality amongst women were highly popularized and revered during my time period. Though the mounting threat became too much to bear when Apostle Paul, who was one of my teachers, joined in on a chorus to righteousness in the name of God. We called each other Apostles, so they differentiated with the teachers of Rabbinical school of thought.

I had 12 Teachers, as the school grew astronomically, I might add. Though I stopped at having a dozen teachers in this new school, just because the turmoil that I had been causing were too much for those other rabbis to bear. Many students were lost to my school of thought and this became a competition to keep those Jews from turning into Christians, as they soon called my form of teaching.

Then all hell broke loose when a certain rabbi tried to have me punished for a crime he thought I committed. One of my students defended me in his own church or synagogue, as they referred to it. This infuriated this particular Rabbi and he thought to soon get rid of me once and for all.

By this time my wealth was accumulating and I could easily defend myself and my school, as a Secular School of Thought. But when this Rabbi, became belligerent and mean to my students at his Synagogue, I had a dealing with it myself. Then an all out war took place with my students trying to defend me and my teachers caught in the middle of it all.

Then what happened next was a young student of mine came to me and revealed to me that he heard of a teacher who did not like my form of thinking, as he was a bit older and knew the Rabbinical school of thought and became offended with thoughts that he did not acknowledge or agree, as we had many arguments surrounding it. Since I am the Authority, as I can hear Our Lord God All That Is, I knew what I was speaking of. Only this teacher called Judas knows of another school of thought that contradicted my own. And as per his experience he couldn't figure out which thought to reveal itself pure. So rather than await his re experience to sort out this confusion within him, he just thought he should betray me and my school by having this Rabbi turn his back against me.

What this means is that I no longer am a religious leader or a member of the Jewish faith, that I have left my heritage and community for good and was to be ostracized by my own people. This Apostle Judas revealed to this Rabbi, that I thought I was a Messiah to heal the rift between the rich and the poor and to combine those who prayed to the Goddess Isis and those who prayed to Our Lord God All That Is. He knew I communicated with the Heaven's Plane and there laid my answers to life's puzzling dilemma. So rather than ask me about this, he betrayed my trust and called me a self confessed Messiah.

Now I am not going to confess that I am or ever was a Messiah to bring these people together. I thought I was living my truth and my life with my wife and children. By this time I had another child Ruth, so named after my sister.

Why was that so threatening to the Jewish faith to be so Titled a Messiah when you truly are one?

The Answer lies in the area of their faith where the Prophet Elijah talked of a man who shall be born to bring together two separate entities under one God. But he had certain criteria that were enacted to be precise and I did nothing to fit into that category, even though I knew what these were. I thought, why should I follow some psychic's premonitions? I am a grown soul who chooses to live the life I choose to have. So, I deleted those same overtures and expectations and re-wrote the script as I saw fit.

This he took to other Rabbis and demanded that I either detract that Title or live up to its expectations. Which I would neither do. Then it became worse for me and my School of Thought where I would wind up losing students and their teachers one by one.

These Teachers were paid off in full of their contracts and let go of my teachings even though theirs made no sense at all to them. In fact, all my teachers betrayed my trust and I was left with a School of Thought that had no students to call my own. Though, they remained with me till the end of time as each generation past, they carried my teachings and thoughts with them until those books I had written in became besmirched by their own ideas and thoughts.

My students dispersed with their parent's affairs with the government, as any new schools were subsidized by our taxes paid at that time frame; while I became an unloved soul who was despised by my own Community. If that wasn't worse, I had lost all my fortunes that I had accumulated over those few years when the School was thriving on its own merits.

I took my wife and children and was about to leave this town when a curious thing occurred to cause me to remain right where I was. I was taken to see a Mistress who had done a reading for me during my younger days, who told me to do a specific prayer so that my soul will rejuvenate me once I pass over to the other side. For this reason, I opted to stay wondering all the way, why my soul would have to be rejuvenated from the Heaven's plane. This time I was too curious to wonder why I would require such an enactment like this.

So this is what occurred. Having no preconceived ideas regarding where my life was going, I opted to defend myself as per my students, who chose to stay with me, at least those who were older and enjoyed my teachings. They began promoting my School of Thought even though all but one of my teachers left my side. I decided to have a supper meeting with some of my older students to whom were my sole supporters, when I had invited one soul, Judas who had no interest in my School, but came to my dining room table trying to save me from myself. He had emerged to be my staunches critic defending the Rabbinical posts and decrying that I am defacing Moses's teachings and that I would be hung by God Himself for turning my back on His people.

This teacher who noted the differences in each thought had offered a post in a Rabbinical church no less and if I take it, then I am returning to the folds of Jewdom. If I refuse, then he and all the rest would ensure that my life would be taken.

I refused to do no such thing. Though I did return to this Priest who called himself a Rabbi and stuck my fingers up my nose and said, "like hell I would take such an imposition. To be called a Rabbi is blasphemous to Lord God All That Is." Yes, I was fit to be tide in those days. I was a young man and was not the lamb everyone makes me out to be.

Then I came close to death when I was torn from my house and taken to another side of the building and beaten to a pulp by others who themselves called Rabbinical students of harm. From here on in, it became worse for me and my wife and children, as the youngest was still a babe and the first child was being taught by my wife at home, as it became unsafe for him to be left out on the streets to make his way to school, as I had chosen a school that gave way to my form of thinking, as other schools began to spurt up just like it is now with the Montessori and the likes.

13

CHAPTER 3

Sunrise of Christianity

I made my way back home in a decrepit state, to the horror of my wife, who suggested we leave ASAP. My younger child was horror struck as well, when he saw my face and asked if I had fallen down badly and rolled down a hill. I tried to remove my shame of letting them get the best of me, so I decided to not run from this town but to wise up and see if I can do some of my own trouble making attempts to coerce those who had beaten me to a pulp that evening. Their objective was to ensure that I would return not to this village town and would seek my welfare elsewhere, as they had enough of my thoughts to last a lifetime, with repercussions galore as a result.

My lessons were widely spread and Christianity became a word that is and was spreading like wild fire. Though I was the origin of this thought, it was to become a religion much later on. In secret, the Rabbis whom I taught told this to younger Rabbis as many had experienced meditations and their gifts while during my tutorials and programming at my School. Some insisted that I be allowed back into the community and revered for having intelligent common sense values and ideas that were uplifting to them and not so depressing, as those of Moses.

It was clear to me that when Moses had written those books, he was not in his prime of his life and he was tired and worn from finding the land that should belong to the Jews. As time past, his writings were less then desirable. Not that I didn't think others had filled in the gap.

Life was unbearable as it was, but now they were thinking they should go to the government to oust me. I found this out from my students, as they were spies for me. Only they opted to forgo that thought. I, on the other had found this idea intriguing. So then this Rabbinical Study Institution had decreed that those who chose to learn with me, would no longer be permitted inside their Synagogues for any special holidays and or feasts days, and they would be ostracized by those same Communities to which had received those transmissions. This caused an uproar within the Community and they banned me from setting foot inside the Synagogue for prayers and such, as I too enjoyed mass and rituals for blessings as well.

Mary my wife, was so upset and depressed by all this commotion that she could no longer tolerate my fears of revenge and chose to leave this village of Judea and take our children with her to her parents in Jerusalem.

Once she left to go to her mothers in Jerusalem, I, in my defence betrayed my brethren to such a degree that I said, "they were liars, cheats and home wreckers, that this faith did not belong to those who study it; Judaism belongs to those people of Jewish descend, just not only those Rabbis who think they own it." This, I told the government that had taken over this land prior to this time frame.

It is the government's business when there is unrest in the community. Race and creed must work and live together side-by-side using the same laws equally, so those who cause unrest are taken seriously. Perhaps I should state that those governments were similar to those that are calling themselves Democratic even though we had an Emperor, Augustus Caesar to be precise, who took over the Roman Empire in the times that I was alive. I had deliberately caused a furor in the Jewish Community by involving the government into their Communities where they did not belong. I desired them to protect my Institution, as it is much better in terms of reasoning then theirs are, even though it is an ancient thought. This horrified all the Jews and they ganged up together to point their fingers at me claiming me to be the king of all Jews and causing a huge turmoil within their people and that I should be punished accordingly.

The governor at this time refused to hear this, as he had heard so many good things about my religious thought and refused to change my position or condemn me for any good cause they deemed fit. So rather than releasing me to their charges once again he suggested I move myself from harms way and go off and live a quiet life in another town where they had not heard of me.

Only I remained. Even though I was given a chance to leave, as that is all the Jewish Communities desired of me as well. They wanted me to leave their homes and families as they are, and not reach out to other thought forms that does not resonate with their teachings, or that is consistent not, with their teachings.

My not leaving infuriated both the governor and his people by now, those who chose to take sides were dwindling on behalf of myself and Christianity, as they themselves called themselves. Those who were Jews feared to take my side, rather than become ostracized with me. They chose to ignore my pleas and my request to side with me, and defend their right to choose which thought is more worthy comparing it to their own ancient thought forms.

Those in the Jewish faiths continued to badger the governor so much so that he begged me to leave or that he could not be held accountable for what they could be planning. He offered to set up my school in a neighbouring Community away from Jewish thought forms and keep my treasury up, so as to keep the school from becoming obsolete, if I had difficulties maintaining students as a result of this brouhaha.

Yes, it was a good offer and I could have accepted it, only it was not good enough for Our Lord God All That Is. He charged that I keep to this path to see where it goes. So I graciously refused the kind offer and advised him that I am here to do a task for Lord God and could not back down regardless of what happened. He chose his words carefully and let me know in no uncertain terms that he isn't going to tolerate further unrest amongst his people.

Having said that he allowed me to take my leave. Further suggesting that I continue to keep a low profile as I had been careful not to get too close to the Jewish Communities' form of thinking, synagogue and such.

After a while when all was quiet down a little, I had a chance to meet another person who should be my support I thought and we concocted a twist so that I can bring down the Jewish Communities form of thought. He suggested that I turn all those who are religious into Christian zealots and raise their conscious awareness into believing that the Jewish thoughts were backwards, old, ancient and outdated. And abuse them by the Romans as many Romans were rummaging through our form of thought just to see what has caused the Jews to become so angry.

When they heard my voice and teachings, they were captivated into my form of thought as though they were hypnotized into believing that I spoke their truths. And their experiences were preferred over religious rhetoric. And the explanations towards their feelings and their conscious awareness became acute the longer I spoke and then they began to notice things occurring as coincidental to the extreme, as though there was a higher power working in unison with their lives lived, and all their troubles were just challenges to overcome.

When they heard this, they were winning over to my form of thought and they then chose to side with me against those same Jews who were nasty and mean to others, who offered to reinterpret their misguided beliefs. All around with whoever they spoke began to comment on my teachings and how common sense I was compared to the religious talks that were offered by their own Priestesses and Rabbis. The Roman Religious thoughts were declined, as the Priestesses would receive new news to seek out male Priests and their counterpart as Our Lord God has taken over the Kingdom of Heaven and Earth.

So they were ready for new beginnings in their religious ideas and thoughts. The Goddess All That Is ruled prior to this civilization and two thousand years before Our Lord God All That Is had taken over, but was slow to cover all those people who had still been praying to the female Goddess. For there to be a balance in this world and others, female energetic beings had to suppress their creative powers so that the male energetic forms could rule to balance out Universal energies between the two sexes. Lord God had ruled for 6000 years prior to this time frame, currently 2006.

Both Jews and Christians, as I would refer to the Romans in that time frame became under my spell so to speak and this was too much for the Jewish Priests or Rabbis to bear, and they came down on me hard and demanded that the Governor do something to squelch my voice. When he insisted that I had freedom to speak to whomever I chose and it did mean those who chose to not listen to me also had this freedom. Then they resorted to accosting me and my zealot students into their form of thinking by arguing things that for sure made no sense to those who cannot hold a candle to my spiritual values and forms of thought.

Once they found they could do nothing to stop me from mouthing my teachings in Public, they resorted to attacking me and my students wherever we went, verbally and physically. The sheer numbers of Jews who had turned against their religion was too much to bear and these were mostly young men and women who enjoyed my speeches and the equality amongst women were causing a rift between service and being served amongst families when all things came to a halt. Not only the rabbis were upset but so were their families whose children remained under my tutelage. I had created inter-marital strife and discourse within families to the point where there were many wayward men and women who were engaged in freedom of sexual expression forthwith. This was OKed with the Romans who were loose as it were anyhow, only this gave themselves permission to become orgy oriented while the strict Jewish thought was for chastity and virginity. Then the uproar became climactic.

The governor could do nothing to stop the anger and resentment amongst the Jewish Communities and its young people and me as their leader. Though many were siding with me i.e. Romans, who say he must be God sent, who else could create so much unrest with a Community as old as these Jewish thoughts were to be?

But still the Jews who now had many people in high places demanded either squelch me or there will be an uprising. How or where this uprising would get created was neither discussed or tolerated. So they chose to have me arrested for the very first time under severe protests by my young and by now wildly exaggerated students who took their freedom of expression beyond what was happening in that time frame. Modesty was revered among the Romans but now they were walking naked everywhere. Especially the women, who chose to hang up their clothes and run wild and free much to the disappointment of those Government heads who were shocked at this total indecent display and had to create laws to support chastity and such, to keep these young men and women's sexual energies in check.

By this time, news had travelled to many areas, town and cities of my thought and the fight between Jewish religion and my school of Christianity as I referred to it. This caused protests and many uprisings within the cities, towns and communities.

Quite a few Romans did not feel threatened by me or my learned ones, who seem to agree with my thinking and many debates occurred surrounding the two forms of thought. Though they had their own, Plato, Socrates to name a few who were similar to my thinking given their observations. They found my thought to be a form of teaching that is aligned with their own Education System and news travelled to those Universities as well, in debate of this new thought that I was involved in.

My writings were given to many. We had news but not a newspaper where all could read, only a few who could actually read news. All news were given by mouth as there could not be much to write about that those regular folks could read. Roman hand written everything and it was too cumbersome to let the regular folks have news, so all was given by word of mouth. My lessons were well versed and recalled excellently by my students and those who chose to listen. Some just heard about the freedom out of context and exercised this freedom however they chose.

I did have a hand in causing an artistic explosion so to speak. As you can see for yourself how many churches have the arts that were taken, drawn and done by my students of Christian faith and teachings. Many Romans enjoyed my speeches of Archangels and Lord God, a bearded white man to whom I could see in my mind's eye. These were depicted everywhere as my stories of these creations of Heaven caused them to imagine the imagery of my heart and mind in my time frame as well. We had what you would refer to as the renaissance in those days as well. Paintings, sculptures and all form of art were revealing the human body to such an extent that those who chose to view them would be gratified in making this art form available to many outside of the Roman Empire.

CHAPTER 4

✦

Crime Against Me & Crucifixion

The arrest was short term, as they had questioned me and decided I was not a threat to anyone. "And having such liberal thoughts, they should be grateful to liberate their sexually suppress people," thought the Governor. The Romans beliefs surrounding sex was not tabooed though some thought it went a little extreme for their tastes. However, "to each their own," they said. Moreover they enjoyed all the flashy outfits that were clearly wide open in style and fashion. Some wore nothing beneath their gowns that had splits down the sides and centre. And when there were any shows of wares, they bared almost all to the public. This infuriated the Jews who chose to wear such layered clothing that one would stifle themselves in the heat at times.

This turmoil lasted quite sometime until they had sufficient evidence of a crime I did not commit. Still those charges continued to be brought up, that I thought myself to be a Messiah that cannot be confirmed due to the legends that they had, which I chose to not follow. When these new charges appeared out of no place that I could confirm. This was brought to the attention of the Governor once again. By this time we were quite chummy, as we had many conversations of the nature of physical reality. He found my knowledge to be quite riveting and fascination. Though these new charges of crimes against humanity were so outrageous to the Governor, that he doubted the validity of them himself. Still the evidence against me and the witnesses who lied had come forth and based on their testimonials they were forced to commit me to these crimes. The crime was that I intended to erase their religious rights and freedom and indoctrinate my own form of religion for the good of all people.

Though that was Our Lord God's intent for my life's purpose. I intended my life's purpose to be just replacing some of Moses' knowledge for the benefit of all those Jews who chose to recall and retell the story of Moses; not to change their religious rights and freedom. They didn't provide a forum to re-evaluate their thought. They upheld all those ignoramus' ideas that to me made absolutely no sense at all. The fact that I had chosen to repair their sexual chakra caused a backlash in their communities when I spoke to them of how those sexual chakras worked, they ignored me due to their own lack of understanding.

Moses himself did not know about this form of system that combined the human spirit with their physical bodies. As is today, we have the exact same issues that are occurring now. Those who gravitated towards learning the Vedas report to us that still these lessons are not acknowledged within the entire world forum, as it is the most intelligent part of humanity's gifts. How it is bestowed on those unfortunates remains to be seen. What this means is, it requires that those who are interested in teaching this system of physical, emotional and spiritual intricacies are blocked at teaching this important piece of knowledge. Lia, you were fortunate to have found a book on these studies.

I at the time, did not acknowledge those crimes and thought that my own religious rights and freedom were being forced upon them to ignore and that they chose to resort to violence in order to bring me and my thoughts down. They transformed my intent, which was to ignore their book of Moses and correct the thoughts that I perceived as a problem. Namely cutting out the sexual chakras and not permitting sexual choice and freedom to reign their religious thoughts. Their power to maintain supremacy in their choices were given to cruel and inhumane treatment of others when the least bit of infractions occurred; for example, a woman would be stoned to death when she had extra-marital affairs but this would not occur to the man if he had done the same.

Why weren't Roman Laws used on Jews, surely to God they did not stone women for extramarital affairs given their liberal attitudes on sex?

That is untrue. Roman Laws were the same as Jewish Laws at that time frame. However, they too denied most of those Laws as Draconian and they were given to ignore them unless someone made it impossible to not use those Laws just to get even with their spouses for betraying their trust.

It just so happened in my time period, A woman was raped due to a student from a Jewish school who thought to blame my teachings for this misconduct, thereby giving those Rabbis a chance at blaming me for his misdeeds. To make it even more obscene, they added that I somehow coerced a fellow into making him believe that it was alright to rape young children in their community as well. Those Jewish clerics, as I am calling them, had no way to endorse how many children were being raped in his community all because of my teachings.

They had this foreign woman to say she was raped by a Christian whose teacher was me, "and he said it was fine that I take what I choose to be mine, without my father's consent."

I was so shocked to hear such calamity that they said I was responsible for, that my own voice was cut, so to speak, and I couldn't defend myself at the time I was required to defend of myself in the worst way. To this day I am upset with Our Lord God for cutting my voice in a time I needed it the most.

Without my defence attorney or my own defence, caused all to believe that this lie was the truth and they chose to ignore my voice later on when I said, "this was fabricated and untrue. I do not teach violence of any kind, least of all sexual intercourse as a violent intent. And those who chose to follow me are the most benign of beings. It is his religion that has him raping this woman, not my teachings." With that, it caused them to hate me even worse, that I would then resort to attacking their own religious beliefs in order to defend my own neck, as they saw it.

When all was said and done, those cleric priests who called themselves Rabbis caused those Governors to re-evaluate the sexual freedoms that I had caused in their own people ie the Romans. No Romans and Jews had raped another based solely on my teachings, as it is not allowed. All were told that it is against Our Lord God to act on violence against humanity for any reason and that sexual expressions be the cause between two consenting adults who had the freedom of choice.

———◆———

For this next part I want to show how this simple rape blew wide open for betrayal of myself, and all those who taught my teachings of Christian knowledge and study.

Those Romans chose to turn my form of teaching to something that was believed to be a bad message for their young people, who chose to hear my teachings. So they formed an alliance with the Jews who swore up and down that I was the most horrible of being to coerce this new unknown knowledge into bright children dissuading them from their elder's thoughts and belief system; thereby, allowing them to discredit their rights and freedoms within their own religious prudence.

They held me accountable with their stories that are now far fetched. Unable to defend myself, as there were too many against me who lied, and were paid exorbitant amount to lie, they resorted to extortionist means to eliminate the so called threat I imposed on their young. This rape began to be something of a loose cannon to focus on. My intent for sexual freedom and their down right disgraceful display of abuse, caused some of my students to flee. Before long, those same students who defended my rights became few and far between. When my students voices were spoken, the Roman soldiers took to eliminating those same students to the safety of their parents. So this man to whom they called Jesus The Teacher, can account for his religious right to be a free man, under the auspicious of the Roman Empire and its Court of Law.

The trial, which included myself and one other person who came to my rescue, did nothing to dissuade those who chose to stand in jury. There were a few folks though not as many as 12. Their Court of Law was inept to say the least, and many could be bought off to side with one or the other party being represented. The Judge could also be bought to bear on those who could afford to have him sentence me to death, as is and was in this case. You will see how much they resort to vilifying me even now, just from this story alone.

So they finally found a way to be rid of me and then they had me tied and nailed to the cross as being guilty of rape and treason against the Jewish faith, as that was the real reason they brought me to justice. Treason against those same Jews who to this day denounce I have ever existed in their time frame. Though many called to say I have existed and I am the 'Lord's Sheppard I cannot want' to be in the safety of His arms. I prayed for mercy, as I felt my flesh being torn apart through which nails embedded beneath my skin felt a burning pain, to which I can only describe as a harrowing experience. They bled me first at the bottom of my feet when they broke both feet, as is what is done to those who have done worst crimes against me. They threw rocks at me, and cheered when I was taken to the cross to be nailed. I did carry the cross for awhile only my broken feet were too painful to bear. I trust you do know one can do most anything under extreme circumstances. Once they found I couldn't carry it on my own accord. those Roman soldiers took the cross from me and hung me upon it once we reached the cross burning section of this village city called Judea.

27

This person Barabbas was chosen to be released rather than me when my final curtain call arrived, when hope upon hope, I thought this would be my chance to resume my words of reason to all those who chose to see me die. I failed in my request to convince those that I had neither committed such an atrocity, nor any student of mine who would do such an obscene act. Case in point, not one Roman student had acted upon their faith but this person is of Jewish faith who would resort to such violence against himself and to me, will pay for his crimes against me. And there I stood, coerced into revealing that,

"I am true to Our Lord God, that I am the Messiah, and if they so chose to condemn me to death, then they had also condemned themselves to death through the annals of time and thereafter, all Jews would be crucified, as I have been crucified by their own hands."

These were my final statements before I was taken to the cross and to be left to bleed on my own until death had taken me. Only that was not to occur. While I stood on the cross my mind and heart was raised up towards the Heaven's plane and when Our Lord God spoke to me, He said, "not to be concerned, for your health is to be restored.

I was taken off the cross; me being Jewish, those learned ones felt that It would be blasphemous to have their own person out on the cross during a sacred time in their calendar and provided my re-emergence from my predicament. They held that with all this blood loss, my reliving would not occur and I would die on the table in a hole in the cliff where they planned to place my body. Only what occurred was that my wife and mother arrived to learn of my disfigurement on the cross, and begged them to release me to their care. This they did without much coercion and they released me from the cross, in the nick of time prior to my death occurring.

With blood lost and their loving hands through which Our Lord God had worked through their hands, as if by magic, they had restored my flesh to its renewed self and so they had me repaired within the end of the sacred time period. To most that saw me rise, felt I was miraculously saved by Lord God as they all prayed in their own way for my safe return to the Heaven's plane. But when I chose not to die, for them to get the best of me, I returned to those same folks that had the nerve to destroy me. I told them this is the power of Our Lord God that restored my life to the same.

As far as my meditation practices went, by remaining on the cross for as long as I did which was two days of standing in one place. I was able to relieve some of the distress I felt in my wounds as most die after a few hours of being bled to death. Though emerging from this fate alive was impossible a task for any man. To those same Romans who saw me walk about after my disfigurement couldn't believe that I would live, remarkable as it was, they called this to be miraculous and word spread that I am truly gifted in religion and should be referred to as the Messiah that I truly am.

As words spread of my re-enactment for my life, I was given full freedom to preach my teachings as any man who could survive a crucifixion deserve to be called Holy. Though the Jews were same as normal, some of them simply ignored me, while others argued with their clerics (not Rabbis, as I do not choose to taint my word on these people who choose the religious route). Those clerics were brutal in their beliefs and approach, told their people to not acknowledge my presence by any means. And to keep their children away from my teachings as it is blasphemous for them to expose themselves to the likes of me.

What about the Jewish people, wouldn't it have been miraculous for them as well?

Yes, to an extreme. Those who were amazed by my restoration occurrence from the cross, swore he must be the Messiah, "you people are wrong to chastise him. I no longer wish to be part of this religion." So those that remained a Jew, knew I was the Messiah and ignored me as per the cleric's instructions, while those who couldn't accept Judaism turned into Christians, as they were knowing who I truly was at the time.

A new religion was born called Christianity with me as the Head for this thought form, its Leader and its source of the All Mighty Lord God All That Is.

I took my wife and my children as they had come as well, seeing it was quite far to return to retrieve them later. They had grown quite a bit since my absence and I told them we would not return here, as these Jewish Communities were to mean and brutal for my taste.

I left to go back to Jerusalem for a time being to be with my family who loved me regardless of the decree. They, my brothers and sisters told me that it is unwise to remain in Jerusalem for much longer than necessary. I thought, where can I go with my wife and children where they would accept my teachings? I meditated on this notion until Lord God suggested that I turn my attention to the East as the Farsis would certainly like a new religion to ponder, I proceeded to Babylon and then to India.

The Farsis were Persians who chose to re-enact their own stories surrounding a Hitler like regime named Mohammed. He was a force to be reckoned with, in those time frames. They were a violent bunch of Humans ever to cross your path. But what they had going for them was the exposure of Hindustanis and their religious beliefs of fairness and love. Even though Mohammed was a vile human being, most were good people who made their living in that time frame the best they knew how.

———◆———

It was a time of peace, relatively, back then, so I took my family back to a few Indian families I knew personally living in India. This was the same place that I learned as a child, the Vedas and meditation. It was there that I formed my School of Thought to which many wealthy children had arrived to learn. A few followed me to India as 'this is the place of opportunity," said so by my Father God. Only a few Jews came with me namely from Jerusalem, surprisingly since they were ordered to stay away from me. Those that came were ancestors of their families relating back to Kind David, Solomon, Jeremiah and Benjamin. These were the lost Jews to whom Our Lord God had talked about returning to their place of origin after the Second Messiah arrives.

Once I arrived there, we had sufficient wealth between us to form a school of thought called, 'Christian School of Learning.' Given that Hinduism is a part of this thought, I thought for sure they would be interested in relearning some of those ideas that were handed down to them from Krishna Murti. To no end they denied there were any relationship to those teachings. I couldn't believe my ears when the Pundits advised me that my form of teaching, though welcomed here, as all thought is allowed in Hinduism, my form of teaching is irrelevant to those same books that I had learned from as a small child.

Apparently, the knowledge I had retained was changed to be updated, modernized and reflective to what was occurring in this time frame. It was modern to the 21st century comparison. That is the reason why they did not see the similarities between the knowledge obtained during the time of Krishna until now, in the time I had lived as Jesus Christ. Krishna had written those books as I understand it.

CHAPTER 5

Life Abroad & Another New Religion

Hinduism accepts all form of thought patterns given that the origin is the Vedas. They were pleased to send some of their pupils to learn new thought.

Whilst I was in Babylon, I came upon a group of Farsis who cherished this man who was treacherous as he is now, called Mohammed. He came before my time and though he had explored religion, his ideas of, 'take all regardless of who you hurt,' was too much for me to not handle. I immediately sought him out and his people and came forward with the idea that he is going to pay for all his misdeeds that he has done once his life was over, as Our Lord God would see to it, that he receives in return all that he has done to others and then some, to which he chose to ignore. Only I had frightened him enough to have him listen to my ideas of thought. Though he chose to ignore me and not offend me by turning a deaf ear to my ideas, unbeknownst to me, his followers were listening quite profoundly to my statements. And for some time they offered to listen some more to a Sermon I was engaged in at the time. Some preferred to see me as a Holy soul for whom come forth to verse out a scripture, so they documented my words and thoughts on the subject, a book my fellow student who is typing these words will revise and document on her own time and effort given.

My Lord Jesus you have committed me to three books now.

I have now committed Lia to writing three of her own stories, one of which will serve a purpose as the true Bible for this time frame to be kept in its purest form for others to use for their heart, mine and soul and salvation, will be kept amongst those who cherish these chosen words of wisdom. As it will be re-written once again, when another Messiah is sent 2500 years thereafter, upon Lia's death as the Messiah and a leader of this next millennium.

Anyhow as the story goes, I in turn offered to write a scripture for their purposes in these lands of glorious kingdoms and wealth. They in turn offered me wealth beyond my dreams and as I lived out the rest of my life here in the old lands of India to which I had travelled to. I became widely known for my works as the Priest from Jerusalem who has renewed their faith in God.

In the old lands of Iran and Iraq, Mohammed soon followed in my footsteps to read and recite the Qur'an as he came to call them. These Scriptures he told others are sacred and to keep them amongst themselves as they are what will bring salvation to all others. Though his life was then over, he held those Scriptures, that I had polished into a book format in Persian and Farsi as the language they themselves had spoken. These scriptures became tainted and besmirched with falsehood and terror. My Authoring these Scriptures were bemused and besmirches as well and all began to believe that they were written by Mohammed. But nonsense prevailed, how can an evil emperor write such a Holy book and live such a perverse life? Once again common sense is lost among them.

All truths must rise out of oblivion, as these scriptures themselves will cause huge furor as I predict as though our Lia has written them herself not. I am the true writer of these words with her amused questions and following my answers. She has removed some of her words, as she prefers that I keep to her own agenda, of not tainting these words with her coming glory. As she is Our Second Coming this I can attest to. Though Our Lord God All That Is resides within her. He is also coming now to be by her side as her husband to which she has waited for Him to return now for 45 years as of 2006. I am including the first 5 years of your life.

It is amusing to me how others have chosen to reacquaint a marriage with a bride and cause it to be known as the origins of my land. One marries a woman not a piece of land. How ridiculous is that I ask you? So you see how besmirched you are all thinking and feeling. I hope.

As for my Ministers and Priest, they too must distort their thoughts and minds and hearts to view these scriptures as ridiculous as it sounds and then to convince others of their validity. It is so much simpler to say perhaps these sound reasoning have been besmirched with falsehood, then to contort one's thinking. Try convincing a child who has less of a reasoning skill without beating them to oblivion and terrorizing these children with these so called thoughts as you have been doing in My name, I might add.

Yes, I am speaking my mind as I have kept silent for so long and watched with horror the crimes against humanity you all have incurred in my name. Those who choose to lead such paths will do so with karma attached to their names for their life lived, and so they too will suffer the consequences of their actions. As I am Our Lord Jesus Christ, here to say to all of you in my church and my religion, it is time to come home. Even this has been tainted with all sorts convoluted thinking. What I mean to say to all of those who chose Christianity as their religion, you are leaving your corporeal bodies and rising above and below whichever the case may be, and return to the Heaven's plane to watch from above or below how the rest of humanity fairs in the End of Times.

Now I have completed this chapter only to begin my continued journey into my past life lived as the Messiah that kept his name as Our Lord Jesus Christ.

CHAPTER 6

Perfection and Misnomers

C reativity is the same up here as it is down there. Though we work on things together, spiritual works is the same as spiritual energy felt in either places, be it on Heaven or on Earth.

Is there such thing as perfection?

Perfection is a judgment call. The benefit for us is that we can know soon after what will become of what we intend on doing, whereas your results occur much later. That is the difference. Though your creativity is not the same as ours since you have only one life to depend on. So in effect we are more perfect then you are, only we are less perfect than the absolute perfection as there is no such thing, since perfection is a call of judgment. As Lia always asks, how can you be perfect when perfection is a judgment and it is unaccountable fact? Though she calls it infinity and unattainable. You can argue that though it is an agreed upon forum, it is questionable to others preferences and ideas of what is perfect, so there is no such thing as perfection, just our own distorted idea of such things.

There is however control. Controlling all thoughts and biases is what we do here on the Heaven's plane as Lia has figured out. That is why she asked this one very important question; why didn't the clerics admit to my time on the crucifixion as a miracle just as all these other plain folks had done? What were they searching for to know that I am and was the Messiah. Why then were they disbelieving?

They were searching for their vision of the Messiah who was an exact replica of Moses himself in the Ten Commandments. The grandiose soul with powers galore. Though I had brought powers with me, they were to change things that were required to be changed and not to be used for show or accidents nor could I use them to assist myself. Those powers I possessed were to be used when Our Lord God allowed me access to them. Hence why I could not bring myself from the cross, as I could have annihilated them using my powers only I chose to defend them against their own lack of judgment. Our Lord God suggested to me that I kill them all. But I chose to discontinue instead, so in actual fact I did save those who I am mistakenly called Jewish people. I am permitted to defend myself until death overtakes them if I choose, just like you had told Thomas he may not instigate but will be allowed to punish those who chastise him for no good reason. And so did my Father say unto me in that time period.

Why are they expecting Elijah now?

They believe Elijah will sound the horn to the coming of their First Messiah only Elijah had already blown his horn with my arrival. This is why all knew my Title. This time there is more fanfare with the arrival of the Second Coming.

I really thought you were going to drop down from the Sky.

Elijah is here to answer your questions my child.

What prophecies did you receive to make them believe you are returning?

When I said that I was returning as a Messiah, it was not Elijah who I meant, it was Lia. Though, when you listen those words seem to change, they thought they heard me say 'Elijah' will return, only I said, 'Our Lia' is returning once a Messiah arrives one additional time.

I remember last year (2005) going to visit my Jewish student. Her son's name is Elijah and she pronounced it, Al-lee-ah, putting emphasis on the 'Lee'-ah. And each time she called for him, I thought she was calling me, because I pronounce my name as Lee-ah.

Still that doesn't explain Our Lord Jesus, why didn't you say Jesus' name, he is the first Messiah?

(Jesus Christ) I can explain my end of this as well and I choose now to reveal to you why they chose to ignore me as the First Messiah. I am not the important Messiah, my purpose were to bring into the One True God, the Romans and cause two new religions to be formed, which is what I had done. Then all will play out in the End. It is yourself that he had predicted. And once they see this soon, they will choose to believe it to be true. Who you are is Our Lia, which sounds like Elijah to their ears, as it did to his ears when he first heard our news from Our Lord God. Though your real and true name on the Heaven's plane is Our Lia, it is known to your family as Kalpana, the dreamer. To us your name has great meaning, as the Enlightened One.

(I was so shocked an unprepared for this revelation and for this reason I took so long to have this published. I should have published this manuscript in 2006, it is now 2020 and I am now publishing this as humanity needs to know and whatever I am to do, is in the hands of Lord God All That Is, I am His Chosen One)

I chose to include this in her book as well as mine this particular dialogue, as it is important to understand that while there are errors that are made when hearing things as words that have similar sounds but mean entirely different things. That is why I chose to ignore those readings, as I knew Elijah had made an error. Now I am revealing to all those who are reading this book. The one true living Second Messiah is our author of this story to whom refused to acknowledge this, though she has been seeing evidence of her new personality emerge as of last night January 14th 2006.

I prefer to be your Scribe.

In 2002, I was called to the Akashic Records for a Reading, through an acquaintance of mine. I was told that I was to become an Akashic Records Consultant. as my career path.

Akashic Records are records of the soul that records our thoughts, words and actions for every life we lived from the beginning. These Records are located in Heaven.

Six months later, I was attuned to the Akashic Records. I was to practice working within my own Akashic Records to heal my current life with the help of the Lords of the Akashic Records, Masters, and Teachers and Loved Ones. On the Third practice session, God spoke to me and advise me of my Destiny, that I am to become the Second Coming of Christ. I didn't take the news very well. I thought what you are thinking now. That I have lost my mind.

Why? I didn't have an identity, career, friends, hobbies, love, all the things that others took for granted. Other than my children, my life felt empty and loveless, so much so that I lived my life vicariously through others happiness. It was too painful to focus on my life. The only thing that kept me going were my 3 children. I wanted to wait 2 years until my children were older and then leave. I just wanted to come home to Heaven. I don't belong here, taking up space, that it was a mistake that I was here. I lived an empty loveless life. So when Our Lord God All That Is revealed to me my Title, this was shocking to me. I remember being in a shopping plaza parking lot I kept thinking there are others more worthy then me. I kept insisting that He choose Neale D. Walsch, or Deepak Chopra, Joel Ostean and Oprah Winfrey to name a few, as they are truly influential and spiritual Teachers, they seem more Massiah-ish to me, then me. Then God said, "what have you done with your life?" I said, "nothing." He said, "I choose you to be the Second Coming of Christ." Then, Lord God All That Is began to show me the Events of this world.

In 2005 Jesus Christ arrived with a gift for me, on Christmas Eve morning as I was lying in bed, Jesus Christ stood beside my bed and spoke to me that he had a Christmas gift for me. My instructions were to sit by my computer at 11:00 in the morning. first Monday, January 2006 and he would gift me his story as Jeshua Christ Also known As Jesus Christ.

I just want to say to you Lia that those two paragraphs will show them those troubles you had incurred and how deeply wounded you had lived your life. To choose to leave your life with 3 children and to leave them behind, surely will convince them that I speak those same truths. You did not say that I had told you who you are, but Our Lord God suggested these same words. And it is with His authority that I am providing this story, as it is time now for all to know why I have given her these truths tonight as she sits and types out my messages.

It is time now to say to all those who are Christians and Muslims that your history is being rewritten as we speak. No longer is your Prophet Krishna, Moses, or Myself are the Messiahs that Our Lord God had sent many moons ago, we are now the past, for the present is rising out of oblivion the true Mistress of the stars, the sun, the moon and all the other branches of reality on this Earth plane of existence and beyond, right through to the solar system. We as men had ruled those same planes, it is time now for the women to rise once more to reconnect our hearts and minds to our true nature. As I am providing prophecies in this chapter until the next millennium when another Messiah will emerge.

———◆———

Mohammed was and is still not a prophet. So we did not include him in this paragraph. He had spent many eons in the dark side of Heaven to be reflective of a life lived badly and to re-evaluate how he is to recompense his life to balance his misdeeds.

Who we are, are the Masters, Teachers and Guides on the Heaven's plane, with our Lord God and His Goddess who rule each and every one of us. Through the Eons of time we descend when necessary and then we ascend once we are finished our task.

Who you are are spirits, within the framework of this body. Only you had forgotten this and believe to be humans who live a life in this body and this is all you are. This is far from the truth and it is a result of this thought that you are damaging yourselves by denying what is your truth, heritage and love of Our Lord God I AM THAT ALL THAT IS, that is being reflected back to you in bizarre contorted forms. This you will learn soon enough after you realize how you have been re-creating your reality to how you see fit and how collectively you are destroying your home planet to where you live without considering what will humanity do once its been destroyed. You must realize that you are all one and the same, though you are not realizing some truths, but the lies you have been keeping to justify your reason for being greedy, mean, uncaring towards others and yourselves.

(Jesus Christ) This I have witness from above. And the state of my religion is shameful to me. All The abuse that have occurred due to your denial of your sexual chakras will turn you into a senseless human being without which love cannot reign.

For the next few years coldness will penetrate your lives and barrenness will be rampant as much violence will be served to those who deserve such calamities. United States won't be there any longer, as a country shall take over its lands and their people will starve as not much food will be provided for them as this is the state they had left in their countries, as all those who had been involved in wars of unfairness and greed will have their just rewards. Those who choose to leave will do so by sickness and in health by those who remain here until the End of Times.

September 11th, as it is known was the time when all things changed and calamity occurred by one human being who had been hijacked by others who chose to claim leadership for a nation that did not vote for them, resulting in wars not of their making.

Unfortunately they themselves are not involved in this karmic endeavour as the karma belongs to the people of their country in and of itself, with or without their direct involvement. It is now up to those who choose to remain, to take back what belongs to them as in United States of America. Given the population lessened when it was in the time of Bill Clinton.

All is unwell though, when a certain Messiah rises and take over her position as the Second Coming of Christ.

I have been isolated and unloved for so long. Going from an insignificant person who wanted to leave this plane of experience to this very important position with Titles, is difficult to accept. For this reason I had waited until 2020 to revisit publishing this book. It was a moment of confidence that I am working on publishing this story and for Our Lord Jesus, AKA Jeshua Ben Joseph, to reveal who I am. I am now coming to terms with this.

Later on is who you really truly are. And she is lovable to us all on the Heaven's plane at least. So not to worry. Your isolation is coming to an end. as our Lord God is soon to arrive.

————◆◆◆————

The dark days ahead approach now at a very rapid pace. This year (2006) is an OK year for all as not too much will occur. But come 2007 and beyond, there will be tidal waves, volcanic activities and rain and thunderbolts struck everywhere, electrical fires galore and all such calamities facing our civilization. As all of us are returning home to our respective areas depending on the frequency of those energetic forms surrounding your lifestyle. Be it rich or poor in gratitude and love or disgust and hatred these are the two energetic forms that will determine which side of Heaven you reside to, return to. For those who are being received by me personally live in love and death is just a resurrection of their soul lives minus their corporeal bodies, as they will return to their home on the Heaven's plane. Those that choose to experience the dark side of life, will return to that area of existence and will not be allowed to emerge until 1000 plus. So really and truly they will reemerge from the dark side once after 1000 years beginning of my life lived once more. We will begin again in terms of calendar year once my birth occurs soon after.

All is new including dates. We will return to our calendars once again. So once our Lord Jesus is born once again, then the time line begins anew. So really and truly they will reemerge from the dark side once after 1000 years of his first life lived in this millennium.

CHAPTER 7

✦

The Rest of My Life
and Prophesies

Now I am continuing with my story where we left off. And that is when I had written the Qur'an and they chose to rename the author as Mohammed because he chose to keep this book to his chest and recommended it for all others as well. I indeed wrote this book though some of you think and believed that he ie, Mohammed had written it, it is not so. I know I might be repeating myself but it is imperative that you all know who the author is for this book. Which is why my accounts and whereabouts are also included in this book and so is the Hindu Bible is listed in this book.

Once this book was written I ventured off to an unknown part of town where there has been not so many wars and made my living there. As I felt now I could relax and enjoy my life. This turns out to be in none other place than Kashmir a beautiful piece of property overlooking the mountain scenery and I built a house there with my grandchildren and spent my years enjoying all that India had to offer. I felt this was my reward for all the strife I had gone through in this life. Only that was not to occur. Soon after there were multiple wars and famine occurred, where I was in the middle of some not so very good people who came to me and asked me for a drink of water. Still I peered out to them with a watchful eye to see what they are doing here

These marauders felt like relaxing at my house under the watchful eye of their leaders to ensure that they not harm any of my children or grandchildren. They asked me, "who am I?" I assured them they were soul spirits of Our Lord God All That Is, to which they said they have not heard of such fantasies. And then they asked if that is all I know, as they were led to me for some unknown reason. I told them I do not have a clue why they are here. I am the Messiah which is the Chosen One from God and if they are here, then it is Our Lord God who chooses to send them to me for whatever purpose. Similar to these experiences you are having at the moment. You do not know who or what or why you meet certain folks, they just find their way to your doorstep.

By this time I had about 9 children and they had wed women and men from different races. Not all were Moses' descendent, some wed their neighbour's son or daughter. It was a happy occasion as I cherished each and every choice. I knew that love has zero boundaries, in terms of race, creed and religion. So I was enjoying these prodigies of mine with multiple colouring of skin. These were my descendants and some of them wed the Indian communities Kings and Queens who were my clients as it were, as they heard of me and chose to have me visit their courts many times. And I would take along one or two children of mine with me to keep me company. Mary was still my wife and the mother of my children's children as she enjoyed them all. She was too busy keeping house when our house was so full.

I earned my wealth being a Courtier as it were and provided a religious forum for my teachings. Only they would choose to call themselves Hindu or Muslims way back then as well. When they heard that I wrote the Qur'an, they cherished me and allowed me access to their own students and children in those courts to teach about spirituality.

————◆◆◆————

One day I was going on my way to one of these castles or palaces as they were ornately beautiful, full of jewels as far as the eyes can see. Rich was the country of India. Our Lord God had blessed them with great wealth when He arrived as Krishna.

I spoke to a guru who had communicated to me that he thinks he is going to hell because he could not permit his adult child to marry this one man who was a danger to him and his household. He told me that this man is a dangerous soul who is driven to darkness and evil as he has killed many men before he arrived into this palace This man to whom he chose was Confucius. Confucius was a king in his own country of China. And he was a driven man, who didn't care who he had killed so long as he had something to gain by the killing. He had amassed all forms of wealth and he had his eye on this man's wealth and took an interest in one of his daughters. Now if he weds this man's daughter, he would behold to him a piece of his land. And so as I stood wondering how to advise him, Our Lord God said to him, **"Allow this man to have your daughter as his bride."** This land that was given to him was called Tibet and he kept his wife there for as long as he and she both lived. To which became the Island of Tibet. As it was an island at that time frame. Then Confucius said he desired to speak to me about all those lessons I had taught his wife. And I said to him, "stop killing these people and pay attention to what you have done to their families and I will teach you all I know about spirituality," as he was nearing the end of his life by this time.

I too was too old; around 64 years of age. I had chosen to distance myself from Jerusalem during this part of my live as I had, had too many bad memories regarding the crucifixion and could not go there any longer. My parents had passed on as news travelled to me by boat and oxen and camel, or however it chose to come. I rarely received

47

news from Jerusalem and chose to keep myself away from this place. I was buried in Kashmir as you will still find my grave site, as it is barely touched by human hands. "Here Lies Jesus' that is all it said. My body was then returned to dust. And here I am. So all those books that are written is completely not accurate regarding my bloodline. There are no lineages of mine as they were all lost. My children wed who they loved. And there were folks who were my neighbours and friends and acquaintances. None of them ever wed a King or Queen from other lands other than of Indian descend. So how on earth can these men find my prodigies, or my lineage? We did not think to mark down, who went where down the line. We chose to live each and every life to the fullest just as you are doing even though you are still not admitting to it.

So now you know my life story, as there are some things to share while all the other details are inconsequential at this time frame. However, what is not inconsequential is my karmic threat I have caused all the Jewish people even in this day and age.

As you know another Hitler like being is coming to power, very soon. He and all his armies whom he is currently amassing, though not one of you know this, as it is a secret, will condemn all those who chose to take Muslim land away from the Muslims, as they are about to rise against all those who chose to keep their wealth to themselves.

This oil rich country Afghanistan and Iraq have been keeping their mouths shut over this time period, only to have them rise up and take over the land that is possessed by the Americans here and there. They are summoning those godly powers to which they have seemingly prayed to over their entire lives for this moment in time and space. This is a prophesy yet to come, that, when the Americans are down on their luck and they will be; will be the time when they are primed for a takeover in their own land and space. A single child will survive from these folks who currently own and live there. As the rest will be wiped off the face of this planet Earth along with the Jewish people who are currently running this war for their benefit. Dick Chaney and the rest of his crew will die a horrible death as will George W Bush and his entire clan of families. All who joined in on this filthy wealth they had stolen, will also find their hands tainted by the same brush so to speak. That includes Canada to some degree. Even though they had their own oil. This oil came in and contaminated your oil, so there will be some backlash as a result. We do have some fears here as well. Canada won't survive either for too long as the turmoil will increase in their temperatures and sickness and all the healthy folks won't choose to heal them any longer, as they too will die, as the SARS had caused them to believe.

Other prophesies are such that those who were involved in this tainted oil scam in Europe will also pay to have it. So much so, that their lands that are currently in use will become so cold and barren that all life will soon disappear as is the case with Russia, though they are cold climate to begin with, theirs will turn to ice as the new lands will become the North pole as there will be a shift in this atmosphere to coerce this planet to roll over onto its side.

CHAPTER 8

———◆———

More Prophesies

This chapter is more than just my life story as it is more about what is to come to all those who survive the next 2000 years. Life will be lived a long long time. This is unheard of for many of you who have lived to be 100 or so years mostly 60-80 years. Which seems to be the norm. Not only will I live to see the millennium, so will the rest of you who are born and survive the turmoil that is to come.

Life on the Earth plane is quiet and restored to its peaceful nature until 2300 years. Shortly thereafter, some of those who were sent to the dark side begin to be born and integrate themselves into the fabric of society. They will create messes upon messes there after, creating much havoc, so that there becomes another war. The next war will accumulate for reasons that are unknown to you with those learned ones who have way advance technologies making what you have downright pitiful. So far they are forbidden by us to enter into this Solar System as there is a law similar to what Gene Roddenberry had portrayed in Star Trek episodes. He is a solar level impersonator, who had been born human so that he can then create an image in your mental framework, the possibilities of humans to explore their Solar System and space in different dimensions of reality.

So now I am giving you the future trends and what you all will be doing. Therefore, births are going to be blessings, as only one child is born to every woman who chooses to have a child. Once that is created, then only this child can have another. Severe population shortages is occurring to offset those living conditions that are pre-existing currently.

Your natural tendencies to join in matrimony will not occur as well since you will be forbidden to marry one single person to have and to hold for richer for poorer until death. Those who choose to believe this to occur will be gifted with many loves in the next century, and those who choose to disbelieve will have one love lost. So for those who choose to have more then one child won't be gifted until 100 years of their lives have passed on. Since you are to live past 2000 years, death will be few and far between. Only those who choose to leave this plane will have death occur to them so accidents and suicides are to be gone by the way side.

As for our Lordship who will be creating this reality for you all to have is not going to remain past her 95 years. She and her husband has chosen to leave, leaving behind all that they have left and created for the rest of humanity. Her youthful appearance is remaining with her until the very end of her life. And then they will freeze her body to keep it fresh so that they can still pray to her for their well being and a book will be left behind for all to have and to hold for richer for poorer until death do them part. Those who choose to remain will speak of her often so that her stories will remain fresh in everyone's mind.

Those stories of hers are to be remembered years after her death and then her life will be returned to her soon thereafter. Once they are sure she has died she is returning 2500 years later to ensure that all her books are well kept and no one has besmirched them. She is once again a Messiah to which she will be known as such so as not to alarm those others who have remembered her from her previous life. We will share her secret name as she is called Celestia, named after Celestine Prophesies a book that acknowledged divine coincidences and synchronicities.

Upon her return all will begin to view life differently and more, more children will be born in her time frame so that a decent population growth can occur. Our Messiah will return after 200 years of life lived after which much growth in technology will occur and manufacturing of goods and services renders all higher spiritual beings as a result of both she and her in the future. This new technology will bear great results for humanity as they will covet the skies of earth, their Solar System and clean up all the garbage this civilization has caused in their atmosphere.

Once this technology is realized, warfare would seriously begin, during her time frame, After which she is to pass over to the other side to assist those who are still living. She is to remain the Messiah here on Earth and on the Heaven's plane with Our Lord God. He is the only one who can balance this power as are you. You cannot have the power without it being balanced.

These wars are of your making not. But you will have no choice but to fight given your spiritual values and the death and destruction will diminish your population growth and back to the basics will reoccur on the Earth plane and elsewhere. There will be pockets of humans surrounding your Solar System as there was in your Star Trek Series, each one, the old series and these new technological types that were working and playing in 1990's television series.

Our Messiah representing Goddess All That Is will begin with the war and then she will leave you to the rest of the re-enactment to which you will fight for her sake and your own.

These dark individuals from another world will be a formidable opponent in the battle for freedom of the skies and space. Entire planets will turn out to be nothing more then dust once they are finished. A new planet will be found that is new with wild life that is wonderment to the senses and eyes to behold such perfect beauty. Then life will flourish once more. With our Goddess's Book of Life on display with copies supplied to all on their view screens and computerized books etc. And then life is to continue. More to come in the future.

Printed in the United States
By Bookmasters